AF269955

OUR
LORDE
AND
SAVIOUR

A guide to the music, life and
artistry of a pop icon

ROBINSON

First published in Great Britain in 2025 by Robinson

1 3 5 7 9 10 8 6 4 2

A CIP catalogue record for this book
is available from the British Library.

ISBN: 978-1-40878-359-7

Designed and typeset by Clare Sivell
Printed and bound in Great Britain by Clays Ltd, Elcograf S.p.A.

Papers used by Robinson are from well-managed forests
and other responsible sources.

Robinson
An imprint of
Little, Brown Book Group
Carmelite House
50 Victoria Embankment
London EC4Y 0DZ

The authorised representative
in the EEA is
Hachette Ireland
8 Castlecourt Centre, Dublin 15,
D15 XTP3, Ireland
(email: info@hbgi.ie)

An Hachette UK Company
www.hachette.co.uk

www.littlebrown.co.uk

OUR LORDE AND SAVIOUR

A guide to the music, life and artistry of a pop icon

M. BARTHOLOMEW

ROBINSON

CONTENTS

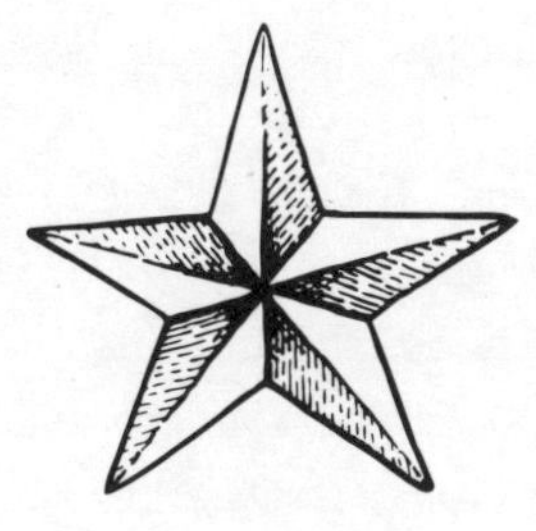

INTRODUCTION

Ella Marija Lani Yelich-O'Connor carved out her own place in the pop world from the very beginning. Ever since she first burst onto the scene as a teenager with her debut album, *Pure Heroine*, she has felt like something different. Her lyrics seemed like they'd been ripped straight from a diary, and her songs sounded restrained and minimalist in a way that was unlike anything else at the time. She immediately received worldwide acclaim and attention, becoming a critical darling with legions of fans at just sixteen. She took the name 'Lorde' from her long-time obsession with royals, aristocracy and the idea of 'old money', and opted to add the 'e' to make it more feminine. She also loved the idea of having a one-word alias, inspired by her pop predecessors Prince, Cher and Madonna.

Whereas some artists would ride the wave of a dazzling debut as much as possible, Lorde withdrew for four years while she worked on her sophomore album, *Melodrama*. Though this album never quite reached the commercial heights of *Pure Heroine*, it was once again adored by fans and critics, building her into a cult pop icon of untold power. She unlocked a unique level of vulnerability and a keen interest in unusual sonics and production that set her apart from her contemporaries and has since completely altered the pop landscape – her spiritual children Olivia Rodrigo, Billie Eilish, Sabrina Carpenter, Chappell Roan, Troye Sivan and so many more all credit her as a major inspiration.

Then came *Solar Power*, a complete shift in terms of sonics, visuals and songwriting style. It was both an ambitious and a care-free project which saw our introspective popstar look outwards to the natural world. It had some brilliant songs on it, but as an album it didn't reach the iconic status of her first two; it felt too alien to what fans wanted from Lorde and was slightly overlooked in the lockdown haze.

The sunniness of that album was followed by another period of reinvention in the form of *Virgin* in 2025. In the years between it and *Solar Power*, Lorde withdrew once again and underwent a period of serious transformation – she went through a major break-up, struggled with an eating disorder, came off her birth control and began to explore the boundaries of her gender. All that culminated in her most raw and unfiltered album yet: a grungy, unclean, truthful exploration of all of that and more.

Lorde's fanbase is one of the most impassioned and engaged in pop today. Many have grown up with her, discovering her as teenagers themselves and carrying her with them into adulthood. Her commitment to her artistry, to pushing the boundaries of what pop can be, have earned her a pedestal in pop culture for over a decade. She's an artist who has been tuned in to the zeitgeist throughout her career, making music that both reflects and shapes the moment. This book will dive into her inspirations, music videos, fashion and every track on all four of her studio albums. Discover the stories behind your favourite songs, hear what Lorde herself says of her creative process and celebrate an undisputed queen of pop.

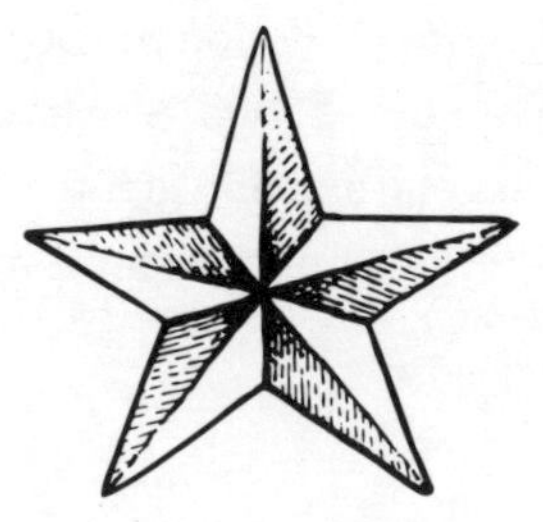

INFLUENCES

To get to the core of Lorde's genius, we first have to look to the multitude of artists who have inspired her over the years. She has an incredibly wide range of inspirations – some who have remained constants throughout her entire career, and some who have had special influence on specific albums or songs.

MUSICAL INSPIRATIONS

'I have such reverence for [pop music],' Lorde explained in 2017. 'A lot of musicians think they can do pop, and the ones who don't succeed are the ones who don't have the reverence – who think it's just a dumb version of other music. You need to be awe-struck."[1] Lorde's respect for pop music is far reaching and palpable in her own songs. She has expressed love for both pop veterans and giants who need no introduction, as well as her own contemporaries.

'I have such reverence for the form. A lot of musicians think they can do pop, and the ones who don't succeed are the ones who don't have the reverence — who think it's just a dumb version of other music. You need to be awe-struck.'[1]

– Lorde

David Bowie, a pop phenomenon in a league of his own, was a huge inspiration to Lorde – and the respect was clearly mutual. His pianist Mike Garson revealed he saw her as 'the future of music'[2] and described her music as sounding like 'listening to tomorrow',[3] leading to her being selected to pay tribute to him at the 2016 BRIT Awards. Her haunting rendition of 'Life on Mars' was widely praised for honouring his memory. Lorde revealed that *Melodrama* was deeply influenced by Bowie, telling Radio 1 that 'It's hard not to make something and not think, "What would David think of this? If I could play it to him, what would he say?"'[4]

'It's hard not to make something and not think, "What would David [Bowie] think of this? If I could play it to him, what would he say?"'[4]

– Lorde

Lorde is also a long-time fan of popstar Robyn, considering her a blueprint for the level of pop she aspires to. Robyn also appeared on *Solar Power*, contributing the spoken solo to 'Secrets from a Girl (Who's Seen It All)'. Lorde is friends with and a fan of Charli xcx, and admitted that Charli's phenomenal success and vision with *brat* inspired her to up her own game for *Virgin*. She's expressed huge love for Katy Perry, quoting 'Teenage Dream' as one of her all-time favourite songs and a masterclass in pop writing. She's also cited Lana Del Rey, Grimes, Frank Ocean, the 1975 and Florence and the Machine as influences. At the beginning of her career she quoted Kanye West as a major inspiration and later collaborated with him on *The Hunger Games: Mockingjay – Part 1* soundtrack.

AUTHORS

Lorde has always looked beyond simply musical inspirations. Growing up with a poet as a mother meant that the written word has always been a huge inspiration to her lyrics, and some of her songs were even originally conceived as poems, like 'The Man with the Axe'. In 2013, she told *Glamour* that her biggest influences were 'Raymond Carver, Tobias Wolff, Sylvia Plath, Walt Whitman and Leonard Cohen.'[5] She is particularly drawn to the confessional nature of poetry, as well as its focus on form and sentence structure, which she tries to emulate with her songwriting.

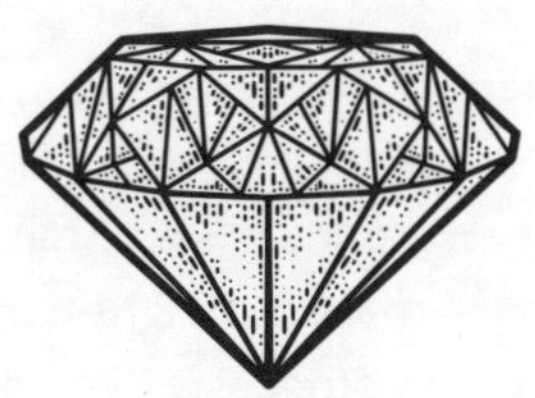

PURE HEROINE (2013):
track by track

PURE HEROINE: you will always be famous. The fact
that Lorde wrote this album at just sixteen is as mind-
blowing now as it was upon its release over a decade
ago. The maturity of the songwriting, the boldness of
the production and the timelessness of its aesthetics
still feel just as fresh and exciting, and it's an album
that only blossoms under the glasses of nostalgia.

When sixteen-year-old Lorde stepped onto the
scene, with her huge head of curls and flawless
eyeliner, she made shockwaves around the world.
The album went Platinum in the UK, US, Canada,
Australia, Denmark, France and Germany (along with
most of Europe), and, of course, in her home country
of New Zealand. She was an overnight sensation,
with 'Royals' echoing on radios around the world

and winning her the GRAMMYs for 'Song of the Year'
and 'Pop Solo Performance' in 2014.

Pure Heroine was co-written and produced with
fellow New Zealander Joel Little – a pop-writing
powerhouse who has also worked with Taylor Swift,
Niall Horan, Shawn Mendes, Sam Smith, Ellie
Goulding and many more. Her right-hand man
throughout the entire process, Little honed Lorde's
unbridled imagination and vision into the confines
of an album. 'She hadn't really written any songs, but
she had all these amazing words,' said Little in 2014.
'So, initially, the process was finding a way to capture
what she was saying with the music and melodies.'[6]

After just a week they'd written three songs
together, one of them 'Royals'. Their collaboration
was a true partnership; Little's focus was on amplifying
what Lorde was trying to say, rather than imposing
his own voice onto the record, and the results were
The Love Club EP and *Pure Heroine*.

Little's sonically sparse, restrained production
is one of the things that made the album so iconic.
The programmed beats, digital glitching soundscape
and spare, bassy throbs use few sonic elements
without sounding empty. It was recorded in a small,
fairly basic studio in Auckland called Golden Age
Studios, where Lorde and Little worked almost
independently to keep the pool of tastes and visions
as small as possible.

What is it about this particular album that managed

to capture the zeitgeist so perfectly? There is
something about it that feels so distinctly *teenage*,
but without ever feeling *juvenile*. Her honesty
is relentless, her coolness infinite and, as many
reviewers at the time pointed out, her restraint
(especially at such a young age) is incredibly
impressive, both lyrically and sonically.

 ## 'TENNIS COURT' 

The opening track of *Pure Heroine* orientates us in the
world of Lorde's newfound fame and her burgeoning
relationship with the music industry as a whole.
Without pretence or warning, she plunges straight into
the lyrics, lamenting the gossip of her peers and fans,
comparing it to watching a tennis ball fly backwards
and forwards across a net. The woozy, bassy synths
and crunchy kickdrum beat drive the lyrical galloping
of the pre-chorus, until the chorus lands with a
triumphant, distorted 'yeah'.

'Tennis Court' does what *Pure Heroine* as a whole
does so incredibly – it gives us an insight into the
world of youth that only a teenager could have, but
with the smart, detached viewpoint that only Lorde
could have. By comparing herself (and the subject
of the song) to classic high-school stereotypes,
she flattens herself to an archetype – the beauty
queen – while simultaneously pointing out how little

sense the archetype makes. The distorted 'yeahs'
and trippy beat make the chorus feel effortlessly
cool, so when the second verse begins with Lorde's
reflection that she'll soon be flying for the first time,
it feels like a sobering reminder of just how young
and inexperienced she is. The derisive laugh and
spoken single-line bridge take us through to a final,
triumphant chorus.

On the ten-year anniversary of *Pure Heroine*,
Lorde celebrated the album in a newsletter to her
fans: 'I'd go on long walks around the neighbourhood,
and began to mythologise the stuff around me (big
empty floodlit rugby fields/bus rides/dark streets/
boredom/isolation) into the motifs that would become
Pure Heroine.'[7] 'Tennis Court' does a fantastic job of
introducing the listener to this world. Thematically,
it introduces ideas of youth, performance and the
double-edged-sword of fame, while sonically it
introduces the essentials of the soundscape that
will come to define the record.

'I'd go on long walks around the neighbourhood, and began to mythologise the stuff around me (big empty floodlit rugby fields/bus rides/dark streets/boredom/isolation) into the motifs that would become **Pure Heroine**.'[7]

– Lorde

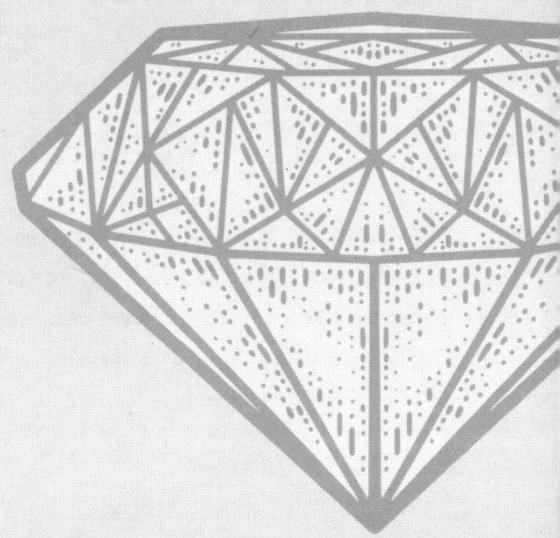

'400 LUX'

The only pure love song on the album, '400 Lux' was described by *Billboard* as 'femme fatale pop at its finest'.[8] It's one of the most sonically dense tracks on the album, with trippy, irresistible drum beats, luscious synths and rippling harmonies.

It's full of gorgeous vignettes of teenage love between a girl and a boy, where the romance comes from wasting time together, driving down the same streets and drinking to make themselves brave. It feels so tender and full of joy, with the refrain of the chorus simply revolving around the confession that she likes him.

The title refers to 'lux' as a measurement for light, with '400 lux' being roughly the amount of light of a sunset or sunrise, presumably the type she watches with her love.

'ROYALS'

Now sitting at comfortably over a billion streams on Spotify, 'Royals' remains the commercial highlight of Lorde's career, even over a decade on. In 2013, the song was inescapable: a radio favourite and a chart-topping success that made Lorde a household name and won her those two GRAMMYs.

Lorde's fascination with aristocracy had already inspired her stage name, so it stands to reason that the biggest hit of her career would also tap into the idea of modern royalty. She critiques the overindulgent lifestyles and larger-than-life personas of modern musicians, particularly in the hip-hop world, commenting on their lack of relatability. She breezes through classic braggadocious staples of wealth and excess, from fancy vodka to tigers on leashes, casting the artists as modern-day Marie Antoinettes, letting the public eat cake.

Rather than being envious of this lifestyle, she seems to find power in her otherness from it. It's not in her blood, but she can play into the fantasy when she wants to. She said of the song: 'I definitely wrote "Royals" with a lightness in mind . . . I was definitely poking fun at a lot of things that people take to be normal.'[9]

The restraint of the production – even more sparse than the rest of the record – feels especially controlled in comparison to the lavish images she conjures of other artists. The backing track is primarily made up of echoing finger clicks, a kickdrum that reverberates like a heartbeat and her own layered vocals almost acting as an instrument. She seems to present herself as the antidote to the wealth and ego of others in the music video; where they rely on signals of wealth to impress, all she has is her lyrics, her voice and very little else to fill out the track.

'Royals' achieved staggering commercial and critical acclaim. It landed on multiple 'Song of the Year' lists, from the likes of *Billboard*, *Rolling Stone*, the *Guardian* and *NME*, and *Rolling Stone* have since put it at number 30 of the 500 greatest songs of all time. A pretty staggering result for a song written by a sixteen-year-old in half an hour during a break at school.

'RIBS'

'Ribs' is perhaps the very definition of a fan favourite – name me a single Lorde fan who *doesn't* love this song. Written about a house party she threw when her parents were away, the song is a palpably taut reflection on growing up, ruminating on the hypocrisies and contradictions of being on the cusp of adulthood.

The waves of synths, like soft sirens, the surprising kick of the drum beat and the choir-like quality of Lorde's layered vocals all combine to make a truly ethereal backing track that purrs like an engine. This is the track on *Pure Heroine* with the longest introduction, with nearly fifty seconds of sounds layering and building before the vocals come in. There aren't a huge number of lyrics in the song. Instead phrases are repeated consistently like mantras, like flashes of memories playing in sequence in her mind: a drink spilling, the song 'Lover's Spit' by Broken Social Scene playing over and over, a conversation with her parents. They all blur into one bittersweet feeling – the fear of getting older.

From the second verse on, Lorde sounds more and more disorientated and unsettled. She becomes more brutally honest – her dreams are turning to nightmares and the streets she used to wander with her friends are feeling lonelier than ever. As the sound builds into the bridge, we feel fully consumed by the vertigo of her dizzying fear. She finally tells us what she actually wants: to go back. She wants to have her childish thoughts and desires back, she wants to feel the freedom of the ideas she had back then. The call and response of the bridge feel almost like a conversation between her childhood and adult self.

 ## 'BUZZCUT SEASON' 

'Buzzcut Season' sounds different from every other song on *Pure Heroine*. With its soft xylophone motif and rippling drum beat, it's a song that builds without release for most of its runtime.

The titular 'buzzcut' comes from the haircuts that Lorde and her friends would give each other at the beginning of summers in New Zealand, a reminder of friendship, childhood and the sizzling freedom of summer. However, the song is slowly encroached by darkness from the news detailing war and destruction, while they try to hang on to their small corner of youthful sunny paradise by the pool. Therefore, the buzzcut could also represent the haircut often associated with the military – a symbol of loss of innocence and identity.

There are two verses before we get the release of the chorus, and when it comes it packs a punch. Something about it feels so heart-wrenchingly familiar and nostalgic – it truly does feel like it lives somewhere you can never go home to again. She keeps reiterating that she can stay in her summer fantasy with her friends, but by the end of the song it's like she's trying to convince herself as much as the listener.

'TEAM'

Even though Lorde utilises the power and uniqueness of her voice across *Pure Heroine*, 'Team' might be the track in which we get the most out of her vocals. As she sings the completely unaccompanied introduction, she sounds as though she's casting a spell on the listener, dragging them into the world of her song. Then her voice twists and distorts as the trademark crunchy kickdrums swoop in and take us back to many of the images she conjured up in 'Royals'. She once again critiques excessive wealth

and distances herself from it, instead aligning
herself and her friends with more natural elements
like moonlight.

The chorus is probably the most unabashedly
catchy, 'pure pop' hook of the whole album. It sounds
a lot 'fuller' than lots of points on the record, with
ethereal synths making it feel cinematic and dramatic;
it's the type of song you'd listen to driving at night
with your friends. Lorde sings about growing up in
New Zealand and being alienated from the dominant
Western culture of America. It's something she
reflected on in 2013 during an interview with *Billboard*:
'No one comes to New Zealand, no one knows
anything about New Zealand, and here I am, trying
to grow up and become a person.'[10] So she wanted to
write a song for herself and for her friends, for
the people who live in these places that never get
shown in movies and TV shows.

'No one comes to New Zealand, no one knows anything about New Zealand, and here I am, trying to grow up and become a person.'[10]

– Lorde

'GLORY AND GORE'

Pure Heroine is so front-loaded with absolute bangers that it has to let up at some point – and that arguably happens around the 'Glory and Gore' mark. It's by no metric a bad song – in fact it's irresistibly catchy and deftly critiques a celebrity- and wealth-obsessed culture. However, there have already been multiple songs that fill that exact role slightly more memorably at this point in the album.

The song presents a fascinating throughline to her future work on *The Hunger Games* soundtracks – in fact, it sounds as if it could have been lifted directly from them. It's easy to imagine the violence and image fascination of the Capitol in the series as the chorus reverberates. A flippant and disinterested Lorde takes us through the hypocrisies of society's obsession with violence, reframing celebrity culture as a gladiator fight and us as the bloodthirsty audience.

'STILL SANE'

In 'Still Sane', the sonics take a backseat, with sporadic choral inserts and drum beats, interspersed with light synths forming the soundscape. It's the lyrics, some of the strongest on the album, that take centre stage, as Lorde reflects on her newfound fame with extreme honesty and nuance. She feels as though she's teetering on the edge of losing herself. She's still finding novelty in fame, in hotel rooms, in working all the time, but she seems acutely aware that it might not last for ever.

The chorus reflects on work and pressure: she sees work as keeping her sane and forcing her to remain down to earth, but it also feels like an immense amount of pressure and focus. The song forces the listener into the tightrope of her existence. She's achieved phenomenal levels of success as a musician and has surpassed her wildest dreams at such a young age – so what comes next? How does she stay herself in this new reality? How does she ensure she's 'Still Sane'? If, as the bridge explains, only bad people want to see monuments of their success, what does that make her?

'WHITE TEETH TEENS'

The titular 'White Teeth Teens' are impossibly perfect teens – always in the right places with the right people. Lorde seems to look at them with both envy and derision. She simultaneously sees through their performance but desires their carefree confidence and effortless coolness.

'White Teeth Teens' is seemingly influenced by

doo-wop music, with swooping peaks and troughs in the drum beats propelling the song forward. As she critiques the idea of the popular clique with this musical backdrop and fifties-inspired references to things like hairpins, we see Lorde call back to the vintage archetype of the preppy cool girl.

 ## 'A WORLD ALONE' 

Pure Heroine closes with ambition. *Billboard* even said of the track: 'A stunning song and ideal album closer, because, really, nothing here is strong enough to follow "A World Alone".'[11] Lorde achieves peak pop here: poignant, gut-punch lyrics with dancefloor-ready sonics. It sits in the hall of fame occupied by Robyn's 'Dancing on My Own' and Charli xcx's 'party 4 u': songs that contain extreme vulnerability while being impossible not to dance to.

'A World Alone' combines two themes that Lorde's explored at length on the album – being on the cusp of adulthood and her relationship with her newfound fame. It's more relatable than tracks like 'Still Sane', which explicitly explores her very unusual lifestyle of being an up-and-coming musician at sixteen, but that feeling is still there. As she closes out *Pure Heroine*, she seems aware that the album will change her life for ever, and there's a sense of both excitement and fear around that. We also, once again, revisit Lorde's fears around growing up. She worries she's expiring and that she won't last for ever; she worries that one day she won't be able to heal and bounce back as easily as she can right now.

The refrain that people won't stop talking, presumably about her, encroaches on the rest of the song, like they encroach on her life. It feels like there's a conflict between the Lorde who wants to dance alone and the Lorde who is constantly surveyed by everyone around her. However, the song (and the album) finishes with the defiant decision to just let them talk – mirroring the very first lyric on the album in 'Tennis Court', where she muses on how dull it is that people constantly talk. By closing the album out with this neat bow, we feel that Lorde has reached a kind of peace: she's accepted that people are going to gossip about her and has decided to let them.

'A stunning song and ideal album closer, because, really, nothing here is strong enough to follow "A World Alone".'[11]

– *Billboard*

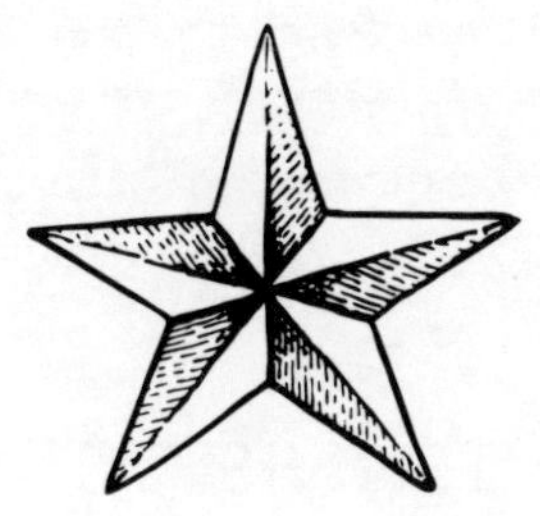

MUSIC VIDEOS

Part of being a pop artist is embodying a whole world beyond your music. It's something that the most successful artists understand, from Madonna and Lady Gaga to Lorde and Charli xcx. All these popstars understand that their purpose as artists is not just to create catchy, good songs for their audience, but to give them something *more*. Whether that's striking visuals, cultural criticism or compelling storytelling, pop music gives artists more space than perhaps any other genre to play with these ideas.

Music videos are the perfect way to broaden out the universe of an album, something Lorde has always done very successfully. For *Pure Heroine*, Lorde produced videos for 'Royals', 'Tennis Court' and 'Team'; for *Melodrama*, she had videos for the album opener and closer, 'Green Light' and 'Perfect Places'; and for *Solar Power* she produced seven. Lorde hasn't really made a single flop of a music video, but here are the top five that are absolutely unmissable.

 ## 5. 'TENNIS COURT' 

'Tennis Court' is perhaps a strange entry for this list as the video is so pared back, but it's so representative of the restraint and thoughtfulness of *Pure Heroine* that it's earned its spot. The entire video is a single shot of Lorde looking directly at the camera, backlit by a throbbing light, and her only lip syncing comes on the guttural 'yeahs'. She fearlessly looks straight on, with nothing else to hold the audience's attention but the black background and the changing lighting. It's such a bold move for a music video and highlights Lorde's self-assurance from such an early point in her career that she knew this would be enough to hold a whole video together. She wears her trademark deep purple lipstick, fishnet mesh top and braided hair like a crown around her head – a simple but iconic look.

4. 'PERFECT PLACES'

Both of the music videos Lorde created for *Melodrama* are fabulous, but 'Perfect Places' just about wins out. The video for 'Green Light' is a love letter to fluorescent nights out in the city, while 'Perfect Places' is an earthy precursor to the videos for *Solar Power*. It was shot in Jamaica and is full of absolutely stunning backdrops – Lorde treks through tall grasses, dances on a beach in the dark, swims and drinks whisky in a lake and swings on vines. The places are as close to perfect as you can get and Lorde wears some of the most gorgeous clothes of her career.

3. 'SECRETS FROM A GIRL (WHO'S SEEN IT ALL)'

Lorde took on a huge project during *Solar Power* – making music videos for seven of the songs on the record. All of them take place in the same world, a nondescript 'island' with a breathtaking beach, cliffs and ocean. It feels very fitting for the album as a whole, and throughout the seven videos Lorde explores this landscape. Most of them don't have a real narrative or plot; instead many contain people doing choreographed ritualistic dances to tie in with the theme of spirituality, or Lorde simply walking around. The video for 'Secrets from a Girl' stands out among the rest for featuring three Lordes, perhaps loosely representing Lorde from each of her albums thus far. She discussed conceiving these three versions of herself in her newsletter, describing the three as 'The Child in her purple lipstick and silver jewelry, big curls thrown over to one side, skipping and bouncing like I did as a six-year-old; The Lover, a baby woman in red with a little diamanté eye, waking up hungover and divine; and The Gardener, me at my wisest and most crunchy, dressed in my own clothes.'[12]

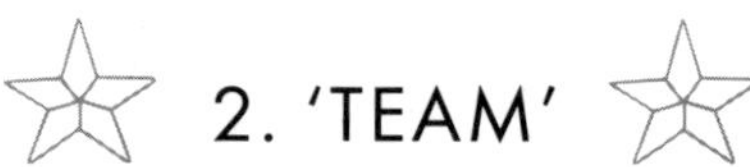

2. 'TEAM'

'Team' is a deeply cinematic music video that creates an entire world in less than three and a half minutes. 'This video was born from a dream I had a few months ago about teenagers in their own world,' Lorde explained on Facebook at the time, 'a world with hierarchies and initiations, where the boy who was second in command had acne on his face, and so did the girl who was queen.'[13] That's exactly what we get – a glimpse into this dystopian dreamscape populated by teenagers. Lorde wanted to create 'a dark world full of tropical plants and ruins and sweat', and the result is a disarming and bizarre universe that blends modernity and ruins, technology and struggle.

1. 'MAN OF THE YEAR'

The music videos for *Virgin* reflect the DIY, mash-up feel of the album as a whole, with everything from the Times New Roman font to the simple video for 'What Was That' pointing to a return to Lorde at her most restrained. 'Man of the Year' is similarly simple, but that doesn't make it any less powerful. Beginning with Lorde wearing a basic white T-shirt and jeans, she takes off her top and binds her chest with duct tape and then moves to a section of the room filled with sand, where she dances and thrusts around. It feels so intimate that it's as though you're watching something you shouldn't. It's unlike any video she had done before.

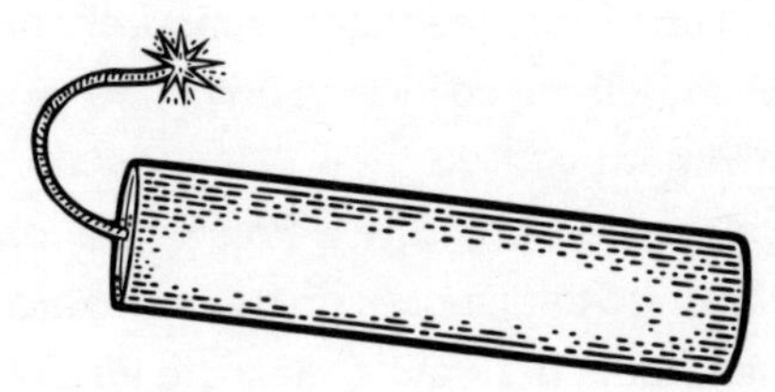

MELODRAMA (2017):
track by track

MELODRAMA is a mythic musical achievement. A Greek tragedy-level dramatisation of a single house party after a break-up, it perfectly captures the euphoria and devastation, the freedom and terror of a relationship ending. It is probably her most beloved work, despite not hitting the commercial success of her debut album. It's the perfect example of an artist growing up with her fans – the fellow adolescents who felt so connected to *Pure Heroine* were now fumbling their twenties with her.

On the night before her twentieth birthday, Lorde posted a letter on Facebook in which she announced *Melodrama*. She spoke about the insanity that had been her last album, how much she'd grown up in the last few years and how terrified she was to 'cross over' and no longer be a teenager: 'All my life I've been obsessed with adolescence, drunk on it. Even when I was little, I knew that teenagers sparkled. I knew they knew something children didn't know, and adults ended up forgetting.'[14]

That's almost exactly how *Melodrama* sounds – a teenager taking frantic notes on the world around her before she forgets her way of seeing it. It's palpable on the album; through the heartbreak and loss is this feeling of desperately clinging on to something, then eventually loosening the grip.

Melodrama marks the beginning of Lorde's collaboration with pop-producing giant and Taylor Swift's right-hand-man, Jack Antonoff. His collaborations are wide and very much fit into the sphere of Lorde's sound, with the 1975, Lana Del Rey and Clairo all having worked with him over the last few years. They worked incredibly closely together; Lorde came to stay in his New York apartment for weeks on end where they would create obsessively. Screenwriter Lena Dunham, Antonoff's long-term partner at the time, was writing her smash-hit show *Girls* there, so two millennial-defining pieces of media were being written under one roof.

'All my life I've been obsessed with adolescence, drunk on it. Even when I was little, I knew that teenagers sparkled. I knew they knew something children didn't know, and adults ended up forgetting.'[14]

– Lorde

'GREEN LIGHT'

Melodrama opens on an electric, difficult-to-beat kind of high. With what is evidently a brand-new direction for Lorde, we suddenly land in a new realm of pop. Gone (or at least changed) is the precocious, distant teenager we met on *Pure Heroine*. Instead, here is a woman that wants, and wants with everything.

From the exhilarating piano motif to the electric repeated shouts and the full-throttle synths in the chorus, this is a new sonic plane. Lorde perfectly describes the post-break-up feeling: the joy of jumping into partying with your friends, the anger and resentment of feeling mistreated and misunderstood, and the constant questions you can't let go of.

Lorde is waiting for the traffic light to turn green – she wants permission to finally move forward, to finally go. It's hard to also not think of the green light on Daisy's dock in *The Great Gatsby*, the literary cornerstone for the idea of longing and wanting. Not only is Lorde waiting for permission to move on, but she's also waiting to *want* again.

'A lot of people we played it to hated it when they first heard it,' Lorde said of the song in 2017.[15] It was received by some as sell-out pop, too immediately danceable compared to the haunting detachment they'd come to expect from her. The song is deceptively complex and it's one that has considerably built its fanbase since its release. It was further cemented in pop culture when it was used perfectly in the US sitcom *New Girl*, scoring the long-awaited reunion of will-they-won't-they couple Jess and Nick.

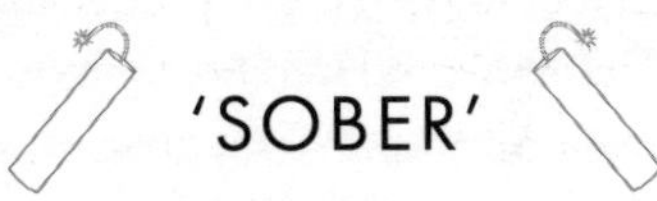

'SOBER'

'Sober' has a sound that consistently surprises. From glitching vocal samples, jazzy trumpets and Afrobeat sensibilities hiding in the electropop, it contains so many contradictory elements that it almost shouldn't work. Instead, it's one of the absolute highlights of the album and of Lorde's entire discography, keeping the electric run going after 'Green Light'.

'Sober' moves forward relentlessly, but Lorde resists the pull with her vocals, instead rippling over the beat and playing with its constraints. The result is a powerhouse of a pop song that explores the feeling of untouchability and power that comes from a relationship and a party in its peak. She describes feeling like she and her lover ruled the world together; that even drugs couldn't touch them. But she can't escape the sneaking doubts creeping in: what will happen when they fall from that high?

'Sober' is the first half of a two-act story that is revisited in 'Sober II (Melodrama)'. This song describes the absolute peak of the party, whereas the second part reveals the darker side of the night.

'HOMEMADE DYNAMITE'

'Homemade Dynamite' is what happens when you meet someone and an epic night ensues. You're lost in the hedonism and joy of the party, instantly bonded with your new companion. In the context of the whole of *Melodrama*, it's likely to reference the same love she discusses in 'Sober', but it could just as well be about friendship, especially as she co-wrote it with a new friend, fellow artist Tove Lo. So perhaps it's more about finding a kindred spirit to party with and the instant, intense connection that comes with that.

Tove Lo's influence on the song is particularly evident in the build of the catchy, rhythmic pre-chorus before the release of the reeling, synth-filled chorus.

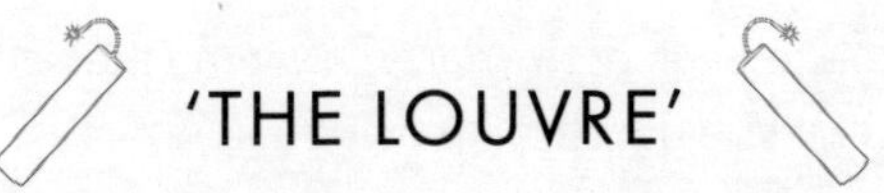

'THE LOUVRE'

In 'The Louvre', Lorde elevates her relationship to a piece of art, worth hanging in the most famous gallery in the world. She reflects on the euphoric rush at the beginning of the relationship when everything feels glittery and invincible: 'I wanted to [give the feeling of] just like the big sun-soaked dumbness of falling in love and it's like your whole head is like glue, it's amazing . . . It's just like this big dumb joy and it's intense – and I feel like the instrumentation in that song kind of helped it get there.'[16]

For said 'instrumentation', Antonoff and Lorde called in beloved DJ and producer Flume, and GRAMMY-winning producer and writer Malay. The song bears sonic similarities with Flume's sophomore album, *Skin*, which had come out the year before. The effect is Lorde at her absolute most loved up, borderline manic in her obsession and passion.

'I wanted to [give the feeling of] just like the big sun-soaked dumbness of falling in love and it's like your whole head is like glue, it's amazing . . . It's just like this big dumb joy and it's intense . . .'[16]

– Lorde

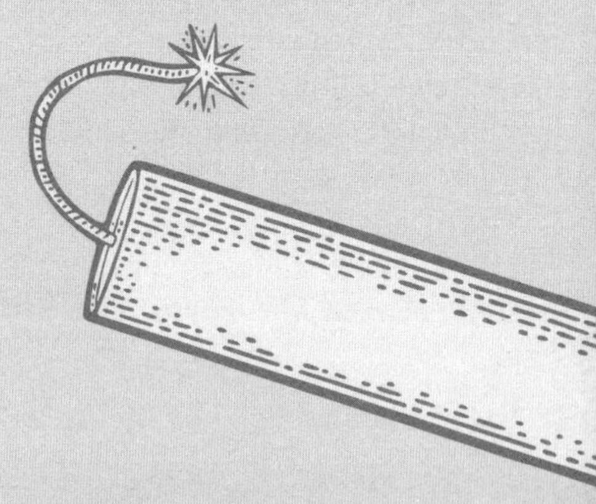

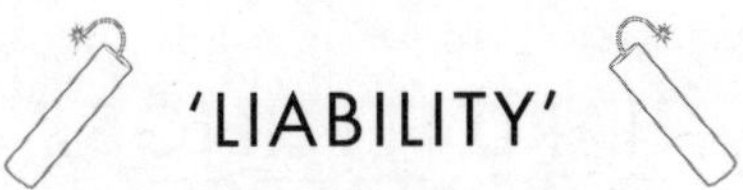

'LIABILITY'

'Liability' strips back everything and lets the lyrics do all the talking. A too-close-for-comfort reflection on feeling too much, 'Liability' pulls no punches with its relentless honesty and vulnerability. Lorde feels that she is the only person that will always be there for herself – everyone else will leave once they realise that she's not perpetually wild and free. Lorde explained that she wanted to write about the feelings you have sometimes when you're alone that are so potent and violent – in the light of day you can normally dismiss them, but Lorde forced herself to sit with them and push them to their extremes.

In 2021, an episode of the cult TV show *Euphoria* opened with a montage of all the highs and lows of the relationship between main characters Jules and Rue reflected in a close-up of Jules's eye, scored to the entirety of 'Liability'. It's one of those iconic TV moments that forever ties a song to a series. Hunter Schafer, who plays Jules, even received 'the sweetest letter' from Lorde after the song was used.[17]

'HARD FEELINGS/ LOVELESS'

The mid-point of *Melodrama* is two songs in one. The first section is a beautiful meditation on the tender calm before the storm during a break-up. Lorde reflected on the feeling in the *New York Times* in 2017, saying, 'I remember this being so jarring while it was happening, like: Oh, this is that moment in the break-up. Until now the two of you were concentric circles, but the instant you get out of this car, you are only going to get farther apart from each other.'[18]

It's an uncomfortably relatable feeling, and Lorde's success comes from describing it with such pinpoint specificity. The 'noise music' inspirations which have been bubbling up throughout 'Hard Feelings' come out in full throttle as the first part of the track draws to a close, with grating, metallic synths imposing on the transition. Jack Antonoff was especially passionate about the finished production on the song, telling *Entertainment Weekly* that 'there's this synth at the end that sounds like metal bending. I'm really proud of that.'[19]

The lyrics of the second section of the song reflect on the loveless generation Lorde's found herself a part of. She plays the role of a modern, detached dater – she relishes the drama and discord of modern romance, in direct contrast to the earnestness and vulnerability displayed in the first half of the track. The overall effect is disarming, drawing attention to the hypocrisies and inconsistencies of millennial dating.

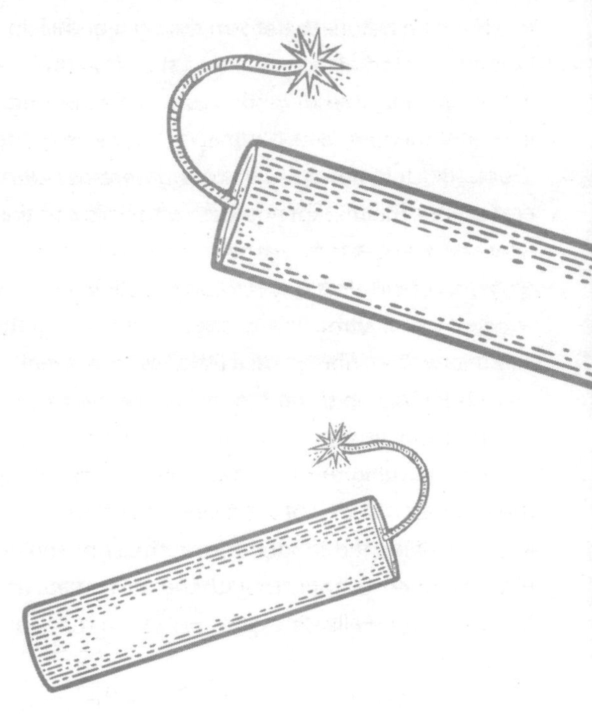

'SOBER II
(MELODRAMA)'

Lucious strings beckon us into the fallout return after the rush of 'Sober'. The idea of melodrama is in full force here, with the song sounding deliciously cinematic through its warm, full strings juxtaposed with trap-beat elements. If 'Sober' is the electric power of the peak of a party and relationship, then 'Sober II (Melodrama)' is the dramatic and painful end point of both. 'There's such a sadness to the lights being on after a party, you know,' Lorde explained, 'this whole room has sort of been washed in this dark, and to see the corners of the room again can always be a little bit heartbreaking.'[20]

Some reprises or part twos can land slightly flat, simply rehashing familiar ground as an interlude, but 'Sober II' is definitely not that. As a pair, the songs show different sides of the same coin, beautifully illustrating the theme of the extreme light and equally extreme dark that comes with the party that runs throughout the album.

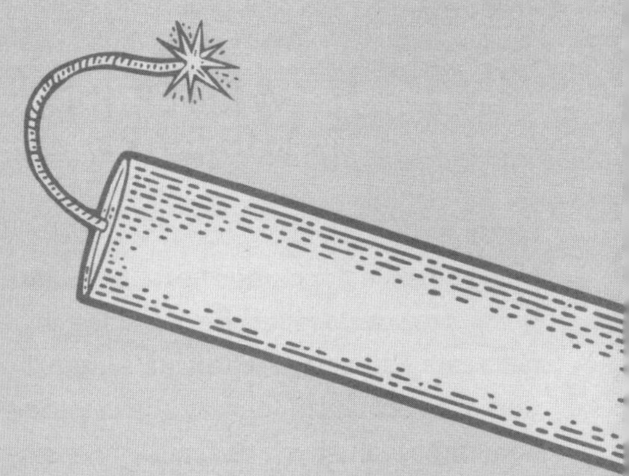

'There's such a
sadness to the lights
being on after a
party, you know, this
whole room has sort
of been washed in
this dark, and to
see the corners of
the room again can
always be a little
bit heartbreaking.'[20]
    – Lorde

'WRITER IN THE DARK'

Lorde has received criticism for being 'pretentious' many times in her career. Partially stemming from being a precocious teenager making art beyond her years and being steadfastly sure of herself, partially because of the way she discusses her music sometimes, and even because of her slightly unusual way of dancing. She once again came under fire for this when a video of her performing 'Writer in the Dark' acapella resurfaced online in which she was shushing her audience when they were trying to sing along. If I'd written this song, I'd do the same – it's a shush-worthy track.

The beginning is as sonically restrained as a lot of *Pure Heroine*, but that's where the similarities end. Instead of isolated drum beats, this is a true ballad, centring on soft piano chords, heavenly vocal layering and building orchestral elements. Lorde uses her full vocal range here, flipping from gravelly lows to heady falsetto. She also sounds more vocally expressive here than in maybe any other song in her discography: it's an angry song, it's a sad song, it's a desperate song, and you can hear all of that in her voice as well as the lyrics.

This is one of the songs most explicitly about break-up on *Melodrama* and in Lorde's career as a whole. Detailing the dissolution of a complicated relationship, Lorde invokes her status as a writer to shame and hurt the person who broke her heart. She won't let him get off unscathed – she will document and mythologise her pain so he is forced to confront it. It draws comparisons with the brutal, iconic heartbreak anthem 'Silver Springs' by Fleetwood Mac, in which Stevie Nicks uses her witchy magic to force the man who broke her heart to carry her with him. Both songs use the power of intense vulnerability as a weapon.

'SUPERCUT'

'Supercut' accesses a similar magic to 'A World Alone': a song that's both perfect for dancing around your flat alone and for weeping your guts out to. Lorde does what we all do after a break-up: she ruminates on the highlights, seeing them flash before her eyes like a montage in a movie of a perfect relationship. She pours all the memories of the magic and love into a 'Supercut', flattening it to the extent that it replaces the person who was actually there.

A soft piano riff drives the melody, with a heartbeat throb and crunchy kickdrum reminiscent of the one in 'Team' hitting hard in the pre-chorus. The bridge – or maybe outro as there's no final chorus – is a repeated mantra of Lorde rewriting what happened. In her imagination, she makes no mistakes and is endlessly forgiving. In her mind, they're still young and wild together, and she begs him to come back into her waiting heart. The first mantra is practically acapella, with Lorde's desperate, pleading vocal hitting hard. Then it builds, with the third and final repetition unleashing an unstoppable combination of full synths and a relentless beat. The sound muffles, like closing a door to a house party as you leave, and the 'Supercut' fades to black.

The song was used to devastating effect in Netflix's brutal break-up movie *Someone Great*. It was apparently chosen before any of the actors were cast, and was in the script from its very first iteration – in fact, the song inspired the movie in the first place. It's absolutely perfect, but have tissues at the ready.

 # 'LIABILITY (REPRISE)' 

If one version of 'Liability' wasn't heart-wrenching enough, Lorde comes back in the penultimate song of the album to twist the knife. Although she once again touches on the theme of being too much, this version is more explicitly about the party that the album revolves around. This is the darker side of the party: the heartbreak, the vulnerability, feeling the rift between herself and her love grow.

The outro is formed from some of Lorde's simplest yet most effective lyrics, as she repeats the simple realisation that she's not the person she thought she was. The party and the break-up have changed her, or rather revealed her, and she must come to terms with not being what she saw herself as.

'PERFECT PLACES'

'Perfect Places' really does feel like the perfect closer to *Melodrama*. The thesis of the album comes together in pop euphoria – a manifesto of a song that you can't help but dance to. Lorde critiques the party, calling out how she craves it, the drugs she and her friends do to feel less ashamed, and how she loses herself in parties to stop herself from feeling alone.

But despite being critical of it, the song really does feel like a love letter to partying, too. The rapturous chorus – with its irresistible hook and syncopated lyrics emphasising every word – sounds like an acceptance of the darker elements of the party. It might be impossible to truly reach 'Perfect Places', but the joy of the party comes from chasing them together.

BEYOND THE ALBUMS

Lorde loves working within the form and constraint of an album. She evidently adores the world-building they usher in and the structure they provide. However, some real highlights of her career are not found on her albums – she's done some incredible work as a featured artist, on EPs, on soundtracks or bonus tracks. Here are five Lorde highlights that you won't find on her studio albums.

 ## 5. 'MILLION DOLLAR BILLS' 
LORDE

The Love Club EP was Lorde's first release, originally put on SoundCloud as a free download to drum up support when she was completely unknown. The whole EP is like a slightly looser, demo version of *Pure Heroine* – Lorde is definitely still finding her feet here, but the songs are strong and it's the release that gave us 'Royals'. 'Million Dollar Bills' is a highlight, a glitchy, catchy, cool, classic Lorde song focused on worshipping money and partying in her trademark sardonic tone.

4. 'HOMEMADE DYNAMITE'
LORDE FEATURING KHALID, POST MALONE & SZA

For this incredibly stacked remix, Lorde stays true to the DNA of the original 'Homemade Dynamite'. The production remains fairly unchanged, with the only major change being three short vocal features from Khalid, Post Malone and SZA, as well as the original first verse by Lorde. SZA's voice specifically is a highlight, bringing another level of depth and feeling to the track, especially when her voice layers with Lorde's.

3. 'MAGNETS'
DISCLOSURE FEATURING LORDE

A slick, sexy and catchy deep cut that's definitely worth the time, 'Magnets' is a collaboration between Lorde and British electronic music duo Disclosure. It sees Lorde self-assured and seductive, singing about wanting someone she shouldn't. It's a peek into an alternative-universe Lorde who is slightly more commercial sounding – the production is slicker, Lorde sounds sexier than we've heard her so far and the track sounds more immediately radio-ready than much of what Lorde had put out at the time.

2. 'YELLOW FLICKER BEAT'
LORDE

Lorde and *The Hunger Games* were two cornerstones of early 2010s pop culture, so it makes perfect sense that she was recruited for the soundtrack. She first did a cinematic, dramatic cover of 'Everybody Wants to Rule the World' by Tears for Fears for *The Hunger Games: Catching Fire* in 2013, before curating the entire soundtrack for *The Hunger Games: Mockingjay – Part 1*. This included the lead single, 'Yellow Flicker Beat' by Lorde herself, as well as contributions from Haim, Tove Lo, Charli xcx, Ariana Grande, Grace

Jones, Kanye West and the Chemical Brothers.

'Yellow Flicker Beat' is the perfect addition to the broody, dystopian universe of the films. It really bridges the gap between Lorde's work on *Pure Heroine* and *Melodrama* – closer to her debut but more sonically expansive and lyrically mature than some of her writing on that album. It was even nominated for a Golden Globe for 'Best Original Song'.

1. 'GIRL, SO CONFUSING FEATURING LORDE'
CHARLI XCX

When Charli xcx released her smash-hit album *brat*, many fans quickly picked up on the lyrics in 'Girl, so confusing' and speculated that it was about her friendship with Lorde. The two have often drawn comparisons with one another, both being slightly left-field popstars with a very specific sound and vision who were working at the same time. They have been pictured together multiple times over the years and were supposedly friends, but 'Girl, so confusing' suggested that it was a little more complicated than that. It wasn't a diss track – it was instead about not knowing where you stand with someone, feeling in competition with other women and how complex the dynamic between women can be.

Instead of being hurt or defensive, Lorde responded with her electric verse on the remix. She let her guard down and spoke honestly about the pressures of famous friendships, her disordered eating and how she'd been projecting strength to the point of shutting down vulnerability. The internet truly did go crazy – it was an incredible moment of pure pop culture in action. *Rolling Stone* put it as their ninth best song of the year, explaining, 'It's the type of honesty and grace that women don't usually give each other in the competitive sphere of pop music. Now that is Brat.'[21]

SOLAR POWER (2021):
track by track

SOLAR POWER is Lorde's most controversial album. It polarised both fans and critics, some of whom praised the bold new direction for Lorde, while some felt this was not what people wanted from a Lorde album and were disappointed by the complete sonic 180. It's a very brave and self-assured step in an entirely new direction – a bold move for any artist, but especially for one whose first two albums are so beloved.

Parts of it work incredibly well. Lorde's vocals on this album are richer and more assured than ever before. Stripping back the instrumentation to a more acoustic sound really allows them to shine. It's also a very well-conceived and largely well-executed folksy, indie, dream-pop album. Lorde was inspired by sixties and seventies psychedelic pop, which comes through crystal clear even on the first listen. She was clearly aware of how much of a sonic pivot this album would bring, saying, 'It'll be interesting to see if this becomes a sound people are interested in because it's so fucking zany.'[22]

The main issue that fans had was that it arguably doesn't feel much like a Lorde album. Admittedly, on first listen, the lack of the explosive electronic production that had injected so much energy and uniqueness into her previous two albums does feel like a loss. Much of *Solar Power* is a critique of wellness culture, or the faux spirituality and the hypocrisies within it, and sometimes it feels like the satire is not biting or clear enough. In comparison with her specific and nuanced takedowns of the worship of celebrity and wealth in *Pure Heroine*, the shots she takes at Instagrammable spirituality feel slightly lacklustre and not fully explored. We know that she looks at it with some derision, but we don't fully understand why that is.

Solar Power was largely inspired by a trip Lorde took to Antarctica. It was something she'd wanted to do since childhood, and after the roll out and tour of *Melodrama* she finally took the plunge. She told the *Guardian*: 'It's as much terror as beauty. You don't feel welcomed by the natural world – I completely felt like an interloper.'[23] That feeling of 'terror', of respecting that the earth is full of powers beyond

our comprehension, is a key theme running
throughout *Solar Power*. The other major catalyst
was the death of her beloved dog, Pearl, leading
to a grief she felt so profoundly it made her want to
focus on the idea of the shortness of life and our
responsibility to other creatures and the planet itself.

Lorde also released *Te Ao Mārama* ('World of Light')
a few months after the record – an EP of five songs
from *Solar Power* performed in the Māori language.
Lorde worked with various collaborators to bring the
translations to life, ensuring that they honoured the
spirit of each of her songs but still made real melodic
and contextual sense in Māori. Marion and Sandra
Wihongi and Hana Mereraiha were just some of the
masterminds behind the EP, guiding everything from
translation to helping Lorde respect the significance
of using the language and adjusting her pronunciation.

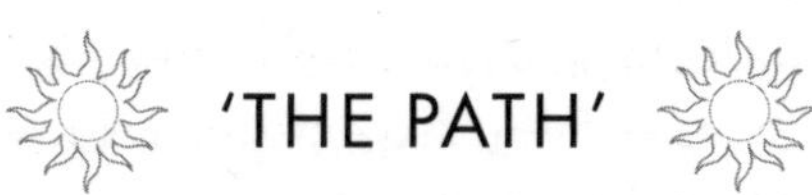

'THE PATH'

Our introduction to the world of *Solar Power* softly
and dreamily presents some of the key themes
of the album – of prioritising nature and rejecting
celebrity worship. Lorde does this by creating an
uncomfortable juxtaposition between her own jarring
modern life – with references to oxycontin, being a
teenage millionaire in the spotlight and going to fancy
galas – and hippie, earthy images of the beautiful

world around her, like the tall grass, a windy island and the changing of the seasons. Her own life seems particularly bizarre and unnatural by contrast. The layered harmonies and echoing guitar feel strangely nostalgic, immediately pointing to Lorde's inspirations of sixties flower-power pop, and work to further this contrast between modernity and nature.

She critiques people who rely on people like her for guidance, asserting that she cannot save or advise them and instead they should turn to the natural world. She sings about people wishing to find salvation or relief or somewhere to put their pain and coming to her, but she's equally sad and complex and cannot provide the answers. She expanded on this sentiment in a newsletter to her fans in 2022: 'There's a lot of trust and faith and reverence based on people in my position, and more so than ever I think I realised that you cannot look to me for the answers. We should all be looking to the sun, the ocean, nature.'[24] In this way, Lorde acts as a mouthpiece for nature, directing people to it instead of to her.

'There's a lot of trust and faith and reverence based on people in my position, and more so than ever I think I realised that you cannot look to me for the answers. We should all be looking to the sun, the ocean, nature.'[24]

– Lorde

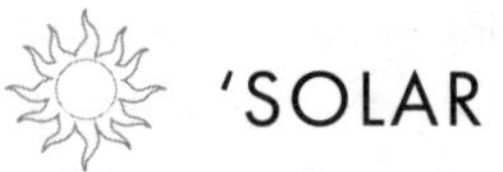 'SOLAR POWER' 

The title track of the album is a playful, percussive celebration of defrosting in the sun after a long winter, and what Lorde described as the 'infectious, flirtatious, summer energy that takes hold of us all'.[25] It's one of the catchiest songs on the album, as well as one of the most straightforward – it doesn't satirise in the way that many of the tracks do; it's simply about the sizzling joy of summer. Lorde herself described it as 'featherlight', but expanded that 'on the surface it's light, but it's got a lot to it.'[26]

The sound is dominated by an isolated, percussive, plucky guitar that adds to the flirty and fun energy of the song. The title refrain of 'Solar Power' doesn't come in until the end of the song, and it's a joyful expansion of the sound thus far. With gorgeous layered harmonies, a rippling drum beat and a trumpet flourish, Lorde lets the full power of the summer sing.

 'CALIFORNIA' 

'California' is about the very first time Lorde visited the US as a teenager. It was also the first song she wrote for the album, carving out a starting point from which the record could blossom. It opens with a reference to Carole King reading her name, surely referring to

the 2014 GRAMMYs when King presented her with the award for 'Song of the Year' for 'Royals' – a moment when she knew her life had changed for ever. She reflects on all the doors that immediately swung open for her and how everyone wanted her, but also the pressure and scrutiny that came with that. She rejects this glitz and glamour, with 'California' itself becoming a metaphor for wealth and celebrity. She doesn't want a California kind of love; she wants something more real and honest, which she finds in her hometown.

Lorde's vocals are a true strength of this song – the increased maturity and richness that can be heard throughout the album are in full force here, with her voice sounding equal parts whimsical and commanding.

 ## 'STONED AT THE NAIL SALON' 

Solar Power does have a stoner feel to it – Lorde herself described it as a 'weed album'.[27] The inspirations of psychedelic pop and sixties flower power align with the idea of having a single called 'Stoned at the Nail Salon'. It's a collection of hopes and dreams, of gratitude and melancholy; it feels like thoughts entering and leaving Lorde's mind and her neutral acceptance of them.

The harmonies are truly gorgeous here, layered

and intense, with backing vocals from Phoebe
Bridgers, Clairo, Marlon Williams and Lawrence Arabia
– incredibly big names to have as backing singers
without major features. Clairo and Phoebe Bridgers
appear on six songs – 'The Path', 'Solar Power',
'Stoned at the Nail Salon', 'Fallen Fruit', 'Leader of
a New Regime' and 'Mood Ring' – but this is one of
the songs in which their vocals pierce through the
most. They float above the simple guitar backing,
performed by Jack Antonoff.

'FALLEN FRUIT'

Lorde was careful to be incredibly clear that *Solar
Power* is not a climate manifesto, even telling the
Guardian, 'I'm not a climate activist. I'm a pop star.'[28]
However, as with any album that takes the dignity and
power of the natural world so seriously, it's impossible
to avoid some commentary on the current state of the
earth and the forces that are attacking its beauty and
strength. 'Fallen Fruit' does this most explicitly,
sounding one part eulogy, one part plea for our planet.

Lorde leans heavily on imagery relating to Adam
and Eve and the Garden of Eden, lamenting the fallen
version of Eden that we have inherited from previous
generations. The planet she admires so much is
already just a shell of its former self – it's already
'Fallen Fruit' – and she criticises the people who

have come before her for their inaction and
destruction. Lorde once again fully embraces sixties
sonics, saying of the song, 'I loved trying to make
it sound like this flower child's lament and making it
sound very Laurel Canyon, essentially.'[29]

'SECRETS FROM A GIRL (WHO'S SEEN IT ALL)'

Many artists have turned their attention to their younger selves during their career – from 'In My Life' by the Beatles to 'You're on Your Own, Kid' by Taylor Swift. It's something that Lorde is particularly well-positioned to do; having been a songwriter and in the spotlight from such a young age, there's a whole bank of her adolescent thoughts and feelings to look back on. This is what 'Secrets from a Girl' does so beautifully: 'I was listening to "Ribs" . . . ,' Lorde explained, 'and just thinking about who I was at that time of my life. I was so apprehensive about what was to come and about growing up . . . this is future me talking back to her sort of saying "It's going to be okay."'[30]

It's a lovely sentiment, which Lorde explores sensitively and universally. It's one of her most grounded songs – Lorde wisely holds back from references to her own unorthodox teenage years in the spotlight, instead favouring more universal images of growing up to which any listener could relate. It closes with a spoken-word outro from popstar Robyn – a genius collaboration with another slightly left-field popstar who's carved out her own space in the genre, much like Lorde herself.

'I was listening to "Ribs" . . . and just thinking about who I was at that time of my life. I was so apprehensive about what was to come and about growing up . . . this is future me talking back to her sort of saying "It's going to be okay."'[30]
– Lorde

'THE MAN WITH THE AXE'

The midpoint of *Solar Power* is extremely restrained and simple. It stands to reason, as it was originally conceived as a poem that was barely editorialised when translated into a song. 'I was very hung over and I think that fragile, vulnerable quality made it in here . . .' Lorde wrote of the song. 'To me, it sounds very private – I sort of don't even like thinking about people listening to it because it's just for me.'[31] It does feel incredibly intimate, with Lorde's voice commanding the song and the accompaniment expanding from there.

It's a vague song and a complex one. It's full of a lot of love and admiration for someone but feels somehow bittersweet. Lorde seems hyperaware of the huge effect this person has on her – all the images of falling in love are also ones of being destroyed in some way, as if the love is too much to bear. She's taken down, she's swallowed up, and she's cut down like a tree by 'The Man with the Axe' – absolutely overwhelmed by love, but also diminished by it.

'DOMINOES'

At under two minutes, 'Dominoes' acts more like an interlude than a song *on Solar Power*. Critiques of the album often point to the songs being quite repetitive sonically and this plucky acoustic track definitely comes very close to a few others.

Almost a precursor to 'Mood Ring', Lorde sarcastically pokes fun at the faux spirituality and hippiness of (presumably) an ex. With references to yoga, Woodstock, flowers and weed, she casts him as a phony, who knocked down second, third, all the way up to fiftieth chances with her, like dominoes.

'BIG STAR'

One of the major catalysts for Lorde writing *Solar Power* (alongside her trip to Antarctica) was the death of her beloved dog, Pearl. She found his loss incredibly transformative and 'Big Star' is a simple but lovely ode to her fallen friend. She wrote about writing the song in a newsletter to her fans, explaining, 'I just wanted to say how much I loved him and how simple it was . . .'[32]

It's lovely to see a dog getting such a heartfelt tribute. Lorde's love for Pearl is palpable on the simple track, as she points not only to her love for him but

also how he connected her with the natural world.
She also calls back to the perfect summers she
introduced in 'Liability' on *Melodrama*, creating a
gorgeous throughline between the two albums.

'LEADER OF A NEW REGIME'

This extremely short interlude is a bleak 'what if?',
where Lorde reflects on what the world could look
like in a not-too-distant future: 'I wanted to have a
little reprieve and go in that Crosby, Stills & Nash
direction a little bit and be like, "Where's it going
to go from here?" Whether it's culturally, politically,
environmentally, socially, spiritually.'[33]

'MOOD RING'

Lorde looks to her 'Mood Ring' to understand how
she's feeling – she's so disconnected from herself
that she doesn't know her own emotions and
needs a fake barometer to explain it to her. As in
'Dominoes', she pokes fun at what she seems to
see as performative spirituality and its constraints:
burning sage and cleansing crystals, doing
meditations and sun salutations do nothing to make
her feel more connected – she still finds herself

looking down at her ring to try to understand what she's feeling.

By just dipping her toe into each thing on this list of slightly hippie self-help things, she highlights the ignorance and silliness of engaging with that world on a superficial level. She thinks that just by burning sage she'll magically be completely changed and feels betrayed when that's not the case.

'OCEANIC FEELING'

'Oceanic Feeling', an ode to New Zealand, Lorde's family and her hazy vision of the future, is one of her favourite songs she's ever written. It's a dazzling high on the album: the most sonically engaging, with wistful and delicate lyrics. She knew that she wanted this to be the closing track, explaining, 'I really wanted it to sound like when I get up in the morning at home and go outside and think about what the day's going to hold. Am I going to go to the beach? Am I going to go fishing? What's going to happen? I wanted to make something that people from New Zealand would hear and would feel like, "Oh, I'm this. That's where I'm from."'[34]

It's a complex song – whimsical and light, optimistic and dreamy, nostalgic and bittersweet. Family is a strong theme in the song, with Lorde drawing lines

between herself, her father, her brother, then on to
 a hypothetical daughter she might have one day.
She sees herself in all of them, with each casting
a different kind of light on herself.

Structurally, it's a strange song, with no real
traditional pop verse/chorus/bridge set-up. Instead,
it's a collection of loose reflections that ripple over
the music, building and bouncing off one another
throughout the song. Lorde plays with the rhythm,
cruising along with it and then resisting it. At
nearly seven minutes, it's the longest song on
the album by far.

'I wanted to make something that people from New Zealand would hear and would feel like, "Oh, I'm this. That's where I'm from."'[34]
– Lorde

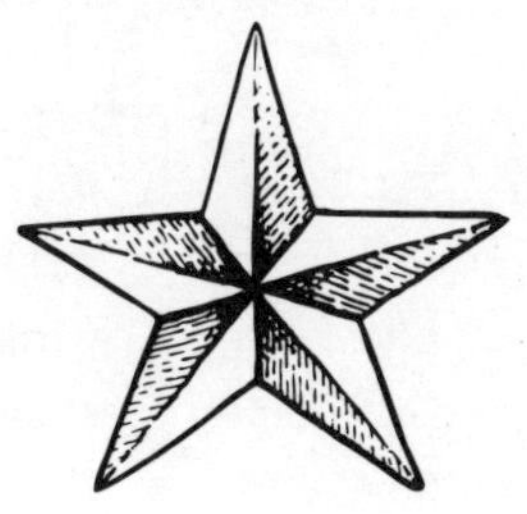

FASHION

Lorde's style has always been fairly understated but still integral to her image as a popstar. It's gone through significant but very organic shifts over the years, and most of her albums have come with a loose 'uniform' of sorts.

Her *Pure Heroine* look is arguably the most iconic. Her dark purple/almost black lipstick, huge curly hair and bold winged eyeliner were the mainstays of every look. All were also painfully on trend, or perhaps created the trend itself, with the Lorde look splashed all over Tumblr alongside the visually restrained album art. She wore primarily black, which alongside the hair and make-up gave her a distinctly vampy look that was a huge inspiration to the 'soft grunge' style of the early 2010s.

Despite being openly sex positive, in the first years of her career she dressed fairly modestly. 'I have nothing against anyone getting naked . . . .' she explained in 2013. 'I just don't think it really would complement my music in any way or help me tell a story any better.'[35] She reflected on this quote in her 2025 *Rolling Stone* cover interview, saying how that had changed over time, and she now found power and value in wearing more revealing clothes. She also commented on how frustrating it was at the time to be used as some kind of symbol of moral purity against her peers who dressed more sexually. Towards the end of her teenage years and heading into her twenties, around the *Melodrama* era, Lorde brought some more colour into her wardrobe. She didn't pivot massively throughout these years, often still donning long black mesh sleeves and high necklines. However, pieces like the fitted rhinestone-encrusted top she wore for the *Saturday Night Live* performance of 'Green Light' in 2017 pointed to a slightly flashier, party-inspired fashion direction. She toyed with those elements throughout the promotion and tour of *Melodrama*, with whimsical outfits like a holographic gown and a floaty, pale blue babydoll dress making appearances.

The most significant shift in Lorde's look definitely came about for the release of *Solar Power*. She adopted a sunny, vibrant colour palette led by butter yellows, pastel lilacs and bright greens. She also debuted her bleached blonde hair at Coachella 2022, fully shedding her darker colour palette in favour of head-to-toe sunniness. Despite Lorde never being a major fashion icon, she's clearly always been thoughtful and purposeful with how she can harness her style to not only reflect who she is, but also elevate the world-building of her art.

Lorde's more recent fashion reflects her relationship with her 'burgeoning' gender identity. In various interviews she has discussed that writing *Virgin* coincided with her feeling her gender 'broadening', and she has recognised more masculine elements of her gender and presentation. In her style, this has manifested as adopting less form-fitting silhouettes, more neutral colours, minimal make-up and more juxtaposition of the feminine and the masculine. She has been wearing a loose uniform of T-shirts, polo shirts and overshirts, and loose but perfectly fitted trousers.

VIRGIN (2025):
track by track

'I WAS TRYING TO SEE MYSELF, ALL THE WAY THROUGH,' Lorde wrote in her announcement of *Virgin*. 'I WAS TRYING TO MAKE A DOCUMENT THAT REFLECTED MY FEMININITY: RAW, PRIMAL, INNOCENT, ELEGANT, OPENHEARTED, SPIRITUAL, MASC.'[36] It's a complex album, at times a confounding album, an exceptionally daring album and a great album. It's not perfect – but it's deeply emotive, surprising, impassioned and true. It has a raw and DIY feel that comes through in everything from the visceral, grungy lyricism to the crunchy, unexpected soundscapes alongside them.

Lorde moved away from her previous collaborators Jack Antonoff and Joel Little for a brand new sound with American producer Jim-E Stack, a gamble that evidently paid off. They co-produced the entire album together, with Jim-E also co-writing some of the songs. They were clearly speaking a very specific creative language, and similarly to *Pure Heroine*, the record benefits from the small pool of voices. 'We would have these moments of discovery where something would be jarring and scary and produce a physical reaction.' Jim-E explained. 'Those were the things we always gravitated towards.'[37]

That commitment to doing the scary thing, to being frightened but forging ahead anyway, is essential to the DNA of *Virgin*. It has an almost unfinished quality to it, but it feels entirely intentional; this was not an attempt at 'the most perfect' album, but rather 'the most real'. This is something that Lorde undeniably achieves – stripping back pretence and boundaries in order to say what she wants to say very quickly and concisely.

After four years away, it's a shame for Lorde's return to be with such a short album – the entire record has a 34-minute runtime – but not a second of that half hour is wasted. Lorde does a lot with a little, blending genres and exploring huge themes of gender, sex, freedom and rebirth deftly and with nuance. The production is riveting, but at times just pulls back when it ought to push further. It flirts with true exhilaration and sometimes achieves it – 'Shapeshifter', 'Current Affairs' and 'David' come to mind – but at times retreats ever so slightly when you wish it would just explode.

'HAMMER'

'Hammer' was the last single released ahead of *Virgin* and was always conceived of as the first track on the album. It opens with a disconcerting whirring sound reminiscent of an MRI machine – presumably a reference to the X-ray on the cover and Lorde's stated objective to see herself all the way through. It's a song that feels like a tightrope; we see Lorde exploding with sexuality and euphoria but also struggling with anxiety and being close to the edge, as well as teasing with her relationship to femininity and masculinity.

Lorde herself described it as an 'ode to city life and horniness',[38] but this is a different city from the blurring fluorescent one she explored in her early twenties on *Melodrama* – it's sizzling hot pavements, getting piercings and feeling like a new person in the same place.

'WHAT WAS THAT'

When 'What Was That' was released in April 2025, ahead of *Virgin*, fans felt it signalled a return to form for Lorde. *Clash* observed that it 'recalls the multi-faceted pop ambition of "Green Light" while refusing to re-tread old ground',[39] while *Rolling Stone* put it on their list of best songs of the year so far in June.

Despite *Solar Power* having some impeccable highs
on it, it's an absolute joy to hear Lorde's voice soaring
over crunchy, electropop production again. It's even
more of a joy when the chorus takes hold and we get
a dance-floor-ready break contrasting with ripped-
straight-from-a-diary lyrics.

'What Was That' sees Lorde in a state of transition
after a break-up and significant shifts in her life and
alludes to her disordered eating. She feels rudderless
and disorientated, unable to face herself, the world
or the ghost of her relationship, instead reeling
and wondering what happened. This tumultuous,
emotionally vulnerable and unfiltered quality is palpable
in the song, with Lorde trying to let it all pass through
her but finding that that's easier said than done.

'SHAPESHIFTER'

An indisputable high on *Virgin*, the third track is
about Lorde confronting her tendency to shapeshift
throughout her life. Her shifting personal identity,
as well as various romantic and sexual experiences,
have muddied her sense of self, allowing her to play
any role and fit any archetype. Sonically, it does a
lot with a little – the almost spoken-word verses, the
unexpected beat and the slow addition of the strings
all feed into the feel of transformation and growth.

On *Solar Power*, Lorde told her past self that

everything will be OK in 'Secrets from a Girl (Who's Seen It All)', reflecting on the fear she used to feel about growing up. 'Shapeshifter' is the *Virgin* equivalent: instead of comforting, it's complex, contradictory and unfinished. Despite looking backwards at the versions of herself she's been, Lorde feels much more in the moment, and her transformations much more continuous.

'Shapeshifter' also contains one of Lorde's most central pillars that she relied on while writing the album: 'We walked past this flyer. I think it was for joining a band or something, and it said, "Do you have the stones?" And I was like, "Whoa, that's tight." I didn't understand what it was saying at first. I know now it's like, do you think you have the balls? But it gave me this feeling that there was a mysticism to it. "The stones" felt like, *do you have the sort of touchstones or the talismans to go there?*'[40] It became a motto for the creative process; when she and Jim-E were tempted to shy away from certain risks, they would push themselves to have the stones.

 ## 'MAN OF THE YEAR' 

The first song Lorde has explicitly written about her gender, 'Man of the Year' is a broody, crunchy reflection inspired by Lorde's visit to the 2023 *GQ* Man of the Year Awards. For the event, she wore a green figure-hugging dress and described feeling completely not herself. It was during the time that she first felt her gender expanding and it was one of the first instances she was able to vocalise it to herself, reflecting that 'being at this event that was celebrating all these cool guys, I was like, "Oh, I'm one of those guys, like, sometimes, when I wanna be."'[41]

The song, opening with only a plucked bass and Lorde's woozy vocals, is one of the most brutally honest of her career. She told *Rolling Stone* how she wrote it soon after coming off birth control for the first time since she was fifteen. Ovulating for the first time in over a decade altered her perspective on her femininity and allowed her to be open to her shifting gender identity. She took a picture of herself in men's jeans, a gold chain and duct tape hinting at binding her chest, which became the starting point of 'Man of the Year'.

The crashing, hectic conclusion to the song really encapsulates this feeling of breaking through, of something coming out that has been subdued. It is an incredibly strong single but is even stronger in the context of the album.

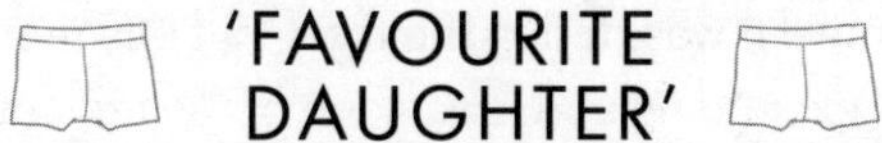

'FAVOURITE DAUGHTER'

In 'Favourite Daughter', we see Lorde broach a topic that she hasn't really explored in her music up until now: her relationship with her mother. She feels at the same time incredible closeness and real, tangible distance from her. She wants to please her and make her proud, but the pressure of doing so can be exhausting.

It's a strangely catchy song for one with so heavy a subject matter, and it's got one of the most poppy choruses on the record. The bridge and final chorus are electric and devastating as Lorde confronts her mother head on, lamenting that her mother never got the acclaim and recognition that she herself has achieved and how in some ways she feels her entire life and career has been for her mother to get a taste of it. As Lorde's mother is a poet, it's easy to imagine the throughline to Lorde's own work and how connected they are through that medium.

 # 'CURRENT AFFAIRS' 

Virgin as a whole is Lorde at her most visceral and physical, which we get at full force on 'Current Affairs'. It contains gritty and coarse lyrics about sex rather than the euphemistic or romanticised versions that we usually get in pop music, which was entirely purposeful from Lorde: 'I didn't realise that I'd been wanting to hear a woman talk about sex the way I was talking about sex in this album.'[42]

The production choices are once again consistently surprising and disarming. After beginning with a very standard echoing bass line, the soundscape builds outwards to more and more exciting places. From Lorde's own vocal sirens layering to the sample from Dexta Daps that flits across the chorus, the elements are in constant conflict with one another but somehow work.

 # 'CLEARBLUE' 

'Clearblue' is a two-minute meditation on the experience of taking a pregnancy test and the dazzling range of emotions that it inspires. In such a short time frame, Lorde touches on the freedom she feels from unprotected sex and being so close to someone, but also on the reality of what the results of the test could mean and the potential of passing on pain that's already been passed down from her mother.

The vocal layering is instantly reminiscent of Imogen Heap, whose influence is evident on the album in the off-the-wall production choices and intense vulnerability. For such a short song, it packs a punch – Lorde herself revealed that she struggles to listen to the song as it's so personal.

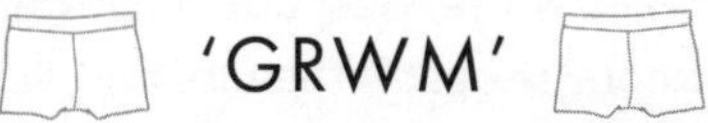

'GRWM'

'GRWM' normally refers to a type of video/vlog, the 'Get Ready With Me', but in the context of *Virgin* it means 'Grown Woman'. It does seem to encompass both, however, as we do see the new Lorde 'getting ready' in a way; it's a song about rebirth and renewal, as well as finding connection to your younger self.

The crunchy, borderline abrasive drop on the chorus is intoxicating, feeling both industrial and disconcerting as Lorde confronts adulthood. She's been looking for a grown woman in the mirror for a long time – after becoming a teenage wunderkind, her timeline was both accelerated but also strangely stalled by her status as a kind of immortal teen. It's also implied that her struggles with food and eating (which she explores more explicitly in the following track) stuck her in a teenage body, but now she feels changed by having the physicality of a grown woman.

The song simultaneously acknowledges the evolution Lorde has already been through while also suggesting that you never truly feel like a grown-up in the way you perceive it as a child.

 ## 'BROKEN GLASS' 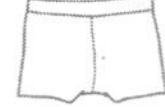

As with 'Favourite Daughter', 'Broken Glass' sees Lorde take on a very serious topic while being an irresistibly catchy song. It's the most explicit reflection on her tumultuous relationship with her body and eating. She explores frankly the addictive element of her eating disorder and the control and power she got from it, but much more brutally takes down everything it cost her – the tears, the sweat, the agony of regaining weight. She wants to grab that version of herself in its throes and shake her, make her see that her weight is not the most important thing in the world and that things will get better.

With an addictive squelching bassline and clapping kickdrums filling out the tight three-minute runtime, we once again see that concision is the superpower driving the album. *Billboard* named it the best song on the record, explaining that it 'may be one of the best songs about eating disorders and body dysmorphia ever recorded, but it's also an A-plus anthem that's worthy of Lorde's upper-tier arsenal.'[43]

"'Broken Glass' may be one of the best songs about eating disorders and body dysmorphia ever recorded, but it's also an A-plus anthem that's worthy of Lorde's upper-tier arsenal. If the entirety of **Virgin** represents a hard-fought reclamation, 'Broken Glass' is its crowning achievement."[43]
– Lorde

'IF SHE COULD SEE ME NOW'

'If She Could See Me Now' starts with Lorde playing the part of an electro-rockstar, her voice gravelly and immediate, and the dirty dissonant synths giving a seductive, femme-fatale feel. It seems to serve the dual purpose of reflecting on how you've changed after a relationship while exploring Lorde's expansive gender identity and her eating disorder. The 'she' could be the version of her that was in a relationship that didn't serve her, or the version of herself that hadn't yet introspected about her femininity, or the version of herself that was underweight and unwell, or a combination of all three.

She takes on the universal feeling of being a sum of your experiences and reflects on all the things that have made her the person she is now. The production on the first verse is so promising, yet the chorus doesn't quite shatter as much as you want it to, with Lorde instead holding back on the sonics and singing in her breathy, higher register.

# 'DAVID'

As always, Lorde takes us to church for the album closer. A gut punch of a break-up song, 'David' takes apart a lover who has clearly hurt her a huge amount. Lorde spoke about wanting to strip back her language for this record after realising that there's power in simplicity and that she doesn't always need to impart flowery lyricism to be smart and impactful. 'David' is where we see this most obviously. Two of the repeated lyrics are so commonplace that they border on clichés – wondering why people choose the loves they do and worrying that they'll never fall in love again. However, in Lorde's voice and amplified by perhaps the most gorgeous production on the record, they feel entirely new.

The self-referential nod to *Pure Heroine* is a surprise delight, as is the ecstatic, rapturous, glitching build that pulls the rug out from beneath you. When she pulls right back, we once again see the sixteen-year-old master of restraint who knows when to go full throttle and when to leave us wanting more.

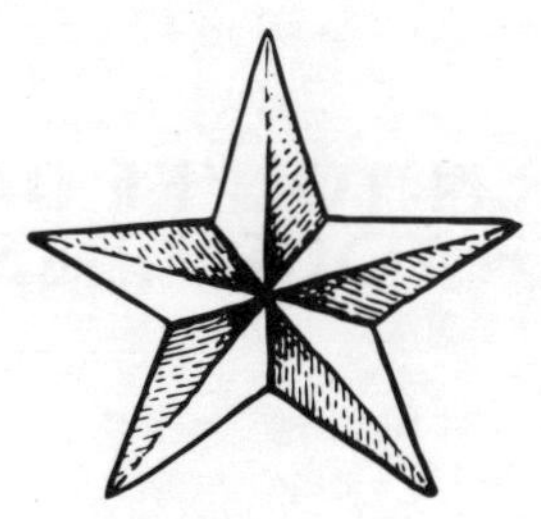

MOOD PLAYLISTS

Lorde has a song for every situation – from care-free dancing with your friends to heartbroken moments alone. For this section, we've compiled five essential Lorde playlists for every mood. It doesn't matter how you're feeling – Lorde's always got your back.

FOR WHEN YOU'RE DANCING WITH YOUR FRIENDS

'Tennis Court'

'Ribs'

'Team'

'A World Alone'

'Green Light'

'Perfect Places'

'Hammer'

'GRWM'

'If She Could See Me Now'

FOR WHEN YOU'RE HEARTBROKEN

'Liability'

'Hard Feelings/Loveless'

'Writer in the Dark'

'Supercut'

'Big Star'

'What Was That'

'David'

FOR WHEN YOU'RE IN LOVE

'400 Lux'

'Sober'

'Homemade Dynamite'

'The Louvre'

'Current Affairs'

FOR WHEN YOU'RE ON
A SAD GIRL WALK

'Royals'

'Still Sane'

'Stoned at the Nail Salon'

'Glory and Gore'

'White Teeth Teens'

'The Man with the Axe'

'Secrets from a Girl (Who's Seen It All)'

'Fallen Fruit'

'Shapeshifter'

'Man Of The Year'

'Favourite Daughter'

'Clearblue'

'Broken Glass'

FOR WHEN YOU'RE SITTING IN THE PARK IN SUMMER

'Buzzcut Season'

'Solar Power'

'California'

'The Path'

'Mood Ring'

'Oceanic Feeling'

ENDNOTES

1 Jonah Weiner, 'The return of Lorde', *The New York Times Magazine*,
   12 April 2017, https://www.nytimes.com/2017/04/12/magazine/
   the-return-of-lorde.html
2 'David Bowie saw Lorde as "the future of music"', *Guardian*,
   22 March 2016, https://www.theguardian.com/music/2016/
   mar/22/david-bowie-lorde-future-of-music
3 'Lorde pays moving tribute to David Bowie after his death, says
   he's her hero', BBC News, 12 January 2016, https://www.bbc.co.uk/
   news/newsbeat-35292034
4 Mark Savage, 'Lorde says David Bowie inspired her album,
   as she releases her new single, Green Light', BBC News,
   2 March 2017, https://www.bbc.co.uk/news/entertainment-
   arts-39143565
5 Jenn Selby, 'Lorde: 16 & already making music history', *Glamour*,
   28 October 2013, https://www.glamourmagazine.co.uk/article/
   lorde-royals-pure-heroine-interview-music-videos
6 Huw Oliver, 'The secrets of Lorde's right-hand man, Joel Little',
   Guardian, 11 April 2014, https://www.theguardian.com/music/
   2014/apr/11/joel-little-lorde
7 Hannah Dailey, 'Lorde digs up "Pure Heroine" memories on 10-year
   anniversary: "Still totally touched by this sweet record"', *Billboard*,

27 September 2023, https://www.billboard.com/music/music-news/lorde-reflects-pure-heroine-10th-anniversary-1235427005/

8 Jason Lipshutz, 'Lorde, "Pure Heroine": Track-by-track review', *Billboard*, 25 September 2013, https://www.billboard.com/music/music-news/lorde-pure-heroine-track-by-track-review-5733177/

9 'Lorde – lyrical influences', YouTube, 27 November 2013, https://www.youtube.com/watch?v=zCSFHsd7NWA

10 Jason Lipshutz, 'Lorde Q&A: New Zealand star on next single, Nicki Minaj & staying mysterious', *Billboard*, 10 September 2013, https://www.billboard.com/music/music-news/lorde-qa-new-zealand-star-on-next-single-nicki-minaj-staying-5687330/

11 Lipshutz, 'Lorde, "Pure Heroine": Track-by-track review', https://www.billboard.com/music/music-news/lorde-pure-heroine-track-by-track-review-5733177/

12 Sara Delgado, 'Lorde's "Secrets From a Girl" music video features three versions of herself – watch now', *Teen Vogue*, 23 March 2022, https://www.teenvogue.com/story/lorde-secrets-from-a-girl-music-video-features-three-versions-of-herself-watch-now

13 Lorde's Facebook page, https://web.archive.org/web/20140115144625/https://www.facebook.com/lordemusic/posts/701802653170791

14 Lorde's Facebook page, https://www.facebook.com/lordemusic/posts/a-note-from-the-desk-of-a-newborn-adulttomorrow-i-turn-20-and-its-all-ive-been-a/1398988346785548/

15 Tom Lamont, 'Lorde: "I want to be Leonard Cohen. I want to be Joni Mitchell"', *Guardian*, 17 June 2017, https://www.theguardian.com/music/2017/jun/17/lorde-singer-songwriter-music-royals-tom-lamont

16 Henry Oliver, 'Spinoff exclusive: Lorde explains the backstory behind every song on Melodrama', *The Spinoff*, 19 June 2017, https://thespinoff.co.nz/podcasts/19-06-2017/the-spinoff-exclusive-lorde-explains-the-backstory-behind-every-song-on-her-new-album

17 Marcus Jones, 'Hunter Schafer on writing Lorde's "Liability" into her *Euphoria* special episode and how the singer reacted', *Entertainment*, 17 June 2021, https://ew.com/awards/emmys/hunter-schafer-euphoria-interview-lorde-soundtrack/

18 Weiner, 'The return of Lorde', https://www.nytimes.com/2017/04/12/magazine/the-return-of-lorde.html

19 Nolan Feeney, 'Jack Antonoff on his jam-packed 2017 and the

Taylor Swift song he calls a "hint at the future", *Entertainment*, 28 December 2017, https://ew.com/music/2017/12/28/jack-antonoff-taylor-swift-lorde-interview/

20 Victoria Whitley-Berry, Michel Martin, 'Lorde on dialing out and turning inward', NPR Music, 15 June 2017, https://www.npr.org/2017/06/15/532599070/lorde-on-dialing-out-and-turning-inward

21 'The 100 best songs of 2024', *Rolling Stone*, 3 December 2024, https://www.rollingstone.com/music/music-lists/best-songs-of-2024-1235163675/charli-xcx-feat-lorde-girl-so-confusing-remix-1235165162/

22 Laura Snapes, 'Lorde: "I'm not a climate activist. I'm a pop star", *Guardian*, 25 June 2021, https://www.theguardian.com/music/2021/jun/25/lorde-im-only-just-scratching-the-surface-of-my-powers

23 Snapes, 'Lorde: "I'm not a climate activist. I'm a pop star", https://www.theguardian.com/music/2021/jun/25/lorde-im-only-just-scratching-the-surface-of-my-powers

24 '24 lessons learnt from Lorde's new album "Solar Power", *Coup de Main*, 20 August 2021, https://www.coupdemainmagazine.com/lorde/17802

25 Lorde, Solar Power commentary, Apple Music, https://music.apple.com/us/album/solar-power/1572940891

26 Lorde, Solar Power commentary, Apple Music, https://music.apple.com/us/album/solar-power/1572940891

27 Brit Dawson, 'Lorde thought Solar Power would be an acid album, turns out it's a weed one', *Dazed*, 5 August 2021, https://www.dazeddigital.com/music/article/53746/1/lorde-thought-solar-power-would-be-an-acid-album-turns-out-it-is-a-weed-one

28 Snapes, 'Lorde: "I'm not a climate activist. I'm a pop star", https://www.theguardian.com/music/2021/jun/25/lorde-im-only-just-scratching-the-surface-of-my-powers

29 Lorde, Solar Power commentary, Apple Music, https://music.apple.com/us/album/solar-power/1572940891

30 '24 lessons learnt from Lorde's new album "Solar Power", *Coup de Main*, https://www.coupdemainmagazine.com/lorde/17802

31 Lorde, Solar Power commentary, Apple Music, https://music.apple.com/us/album/solar-power/1572940891

32 '24 lessons learnt from Lorde's new album "Solar Power', *Coup de Main*, https://www.coupdemainmagazine.com/lorde/17802

33 Lorde, Solar Power commentary, Apple Music, https://music.apple.com/us/album/solar-power/1572940891

34 Lorde, Solar Power commentary, Apple Music, https://music.apple.com/us/album/solar-power/1572940891

35 N. Brown, 'Lorde on being sex positive: "I have nothing against anyone getting naked"', *Vibe*, 18 December 2013, https://www.vibe.com/features/vixen/lorde-on-being-sex-positive-i-have-nothing-against-anyone-getting-naked-294621/

36 Nina Corcoran, 'Lorde Announces New Album *Virgin*', *Pitchfork, 30 April 2025*, https://pitchfork.com/news/lorde-announces-new-album-virgin/

37 Josiah Gogarty, 'Meet Jim-E Stack, the producer behind all of your favourite music of 2025', *GQ, 29 May 2025*, https://www.gq-magazine.co.uk/article/jim-e-stack-interview-2025

38 Lorde, 'Hammer. Last song before Virgin . . .', *X, 18 June 2025*, https://x.com/lorde/status/1935437154378989851

39 Robin Murray, 'Lorde's 'What Was That' Is An Act Of Pop Re-Connection', *Clash, 24 April 2025*, https://www.clashmusic.com/reviews/lordes-what-was-that-is-an-act-of-pop-re-connection/

40 Maraya Fisher, '"The magic lives close to the edge": Lorde and artist Martine Syms on the beauty of the self', *Document, 1 May 2025*, https://www.documentjournal.com/2025/05/the-magic-lives-close-to-the-edge-lorde-and-artist-martine-syms-on-the-beauty-of-the-self/

41 triple j, 'Lorde on 'Man Of The Year', collaborating with Jim-E Stack & 'Virgin' album teasers', *triple j radio, 29 May 2025* https://www.youtube.com/watch?v=aiZ3YxqNvQ8

42 Lucy Smith, 'Lorde breaks down new album 'Virgin': shapeshifting, intimacy & womanhood', *triple j radio, 27 June 2025*, https://www.youtube.com/watch?v=ndPn-pznykE

43 Jason Lipshutz, 'Lorde's 'Virgin': All 11 Tracks Ranked', *Billboard, 28 June 2025*, https://www.billboard.com/lists/lorde-virgin-best-songs-ranked-review/broken-glass/